Fivemiletow

TOM PAULIN

Fivemiletown

faber and faber

First published in 1987
by Faber and Faber Limited
3 Queen Square London WC1N 3AU
Reissued in 2001

Printed in Italy

A CIP record for this book is
available from the British Library

ISBN 0–571–21018–x

2 4 6 8 10 9 7 5 3 1

For Reginald and Jacqueline Weir

Acknowledgements

Some of these poems have appeared in: *Honest Ulsterman, London Review of Books, North, Observer, Poetry Review, The Irish Times, The Times Literary Supplement*, 'Meridian' (BBC World Service). 'André Chénier', 'Symbolum', 'Voronezh' and 'Last Statement' were included in *The Faber Book of Political Verse*. The lines beginning 'Thebes has seven gates' and the chorus 'There are many wonders on this earth' originally appeared in my version of *Antigone, The Riot Act*. I am deeply indebted to Elizabeth Boa, Steve Giles, Judith Jesch, Elisabeth and Thorlac Turville-Petre, Hamish Reid, Ann Pasternak Slater and Gudrun Sowerby for translating texts by Anna Akhmatova, Paul Celan, Simon Dach, Martin Heidegger, and August Strindberg.

Contents

The Bungalow on the Unapproved Road 1
'God Made the Catholics and the Armalite
    Made Us Equal' 2
An English Writer on the French Revolution 3
The Red Handshake 4
André Chénier 5
Waftage: An Irregular Ode 6
Peacetime 9
Now for the Orange Card 10
The Maiden That Is Makeless 12
The House of Jacob from a People of Strange
    Language 14
Fivemiletown 15
Defenester 18
Rosetta Stone 19
Symbolum 20
Jefferson's Virginia 21
Calque 23
Were the Rosenbergs Framed with a Pack of Jello? 24
Voronezh 25
Mythologies 26
Where's this Big River Come From? 28
'There are many wonders on this earth' 29
Breez Marine 30
I Am Nature 32
11/11/84 35
Last Statement 37
Mount Stewart 38
Sure I'm a Cheat Aren't We All? 40
An Ulster Unionist Walks the Streets of London 42
From *Landsflykt* 44
Why The Good Lord Must Persecute Me 46

Really Naff 48
Are Those F-111s? 50
Chucking it Away 52
The Defenestration of Hillsborough 54
The Caravans on Lüneberg Heath 55

Notes to poems 67

Thebes has seven gates
and the sun shines on each one:
just take a look
at the triangle
and the compasses —
dead clear they are,
like an open book.

The Bungalow on the Unapproved Road

The mattress on their bed
was so spongy
we fell all night
into a cut-price nothing
that wrecked our backs.
The headboard was padded
with black vinyl –
just the ugliest thing
I'd seen in a long time,
though the new wallpaper
they'd bought in Wellworths –
tequila sunsets
on the Costa Brava –
might take the biscuit.
That May morning
I looked out at the Bluestacks
and the Glen River –
a wet, chittering
smash of light
where a black Vauxhall
jeuked round a bend
on jammy springs,
like a patched Oldsmobile
heading for Donegal
with a raft of hooch in the trunk.

'God Made the Catholics and the
Armalite Made Us Equal'

The round tables
and vines
under Fabrizzio's glass dome
look newer this evening
because we're met by accident
a long way from home.
It's the far north of Ireland,
a city with walls
and barely a tree growing –
I've come over the hills,
they've crossed rivers,
to hear a formal slegging
in our own accents.
I can't trust her
or her husband,
though now we're talking
about good and bad lines
as if nothing had happened.

An English Writer on the French Revolution

His book is dedicated
to certain ladies –
Mrs John Rae
and Mrs Clive Street
who compiled the index
and served tea
under a damson tree.
He tells us that Barère
was left-handed
and owned a small library
of Chinese pornography
which he called
mon cabinet noir.
He tells us the exact size
of Fouquier-Tinville's
ear trumpet,
argues that Chénier
was a foot taller
than his brother
and describes the operation
on the Dauphin's foreskin.
He is building a bridge
from here to Betelgeuse –
a bridge of damson stones,
tin trumpets
and left testicles.
I sit under my vine
and read him gently.

The Red Handshake

Maybe if I could scrape the earth
from off that ridge where the Third Force
melted out of *The Tain* one Antrim night,
I'd find a man called Bowden Beggs
wrapped in black plastic, like a growbag,
and breathing 'Mind, it can get no worse'?

André Chénier

(Marina Tsvetayeva)

André Chénier climbed up the ladder.
What a sin to be alive!
Iron, iron and cordite, these days
And a burnt tenor.

What father would cut the collar
From his son's shirt?
There are times the daylight's a quick terror
And no one living looks quite human.

4 April 1918

Waftage: An Irregular Ode

All my mates
were out of town
that lunk July
and though we shared a bed still
it was over.
She'd paid the rent
till August first
so each bum hour
those rooms chucked back at me
this boxed-up, gummy warmth
like a pollack's head and eye
wedged in an ironstone wall.
Most every day
she'd paint
in the loft above the stables
while I wandered
right through Le Carré –
Murder of Quality
was where I started.
That dower-house,
it felt like a forced holiday
or some queer, white theatre
open but empty
on the Sabbath.

At night we'd mount
this slippy mime
called *Boffe de politesse* –
we did it best
in the bath, I reckon –
a kind of maritime
bored experiment,

all yompy farts
and soap torpedoes.
One dayclean, though,
when a pouter-dove
was crooling
like a soft hoor,
I thought how James Fenton
read Shakespeare in Saigon –
got the complete works
in dime paperbacks
on the black market.
Bit by bit he'd foreground
the subterfugue text
within the text itself,
and so turn wiser –
aye, I used think wiser –
than us boneheads here.

It was quiet
in the Circus;
Bill Haydon wafted
down a corridor . . .
for a geg one day
I bought this tin
of panties coloured
like the Union Jack,
but she slung it in the bin
and never breathed
the least bit sigh.
'Va-t'en!' she spat,
'I just can't stand you.
No one can.
Your breath stinks
and your taste
it's simply foul –

like that accent.
Please don't come slouching
near my bed again.'
So, real cool, I growled
'Lady, no way you'll walk
right over *me*.'
Dead on. I chucked her then.

Peacetime

We moved house
in '63.

My brother cried
quietly in his room.

Stuff in the loft,
my dad said burn it.

I cut the brass buttons
from his khaki tunic,

sploshed petrol,
felt in the back pocket

of the heavy trousers –
no wallet,

only four sheets
of folded bog-roll

(he'd been an officer
and planned ahead).

I chucked a match.
Whap!

Now for the Orange Card

This might be a french letter –
enlightened, protestant,
and *juste*.
Under the signature
you'll find a small sign;
maybe the man who snicked it
was a mason
wanting to express *freedom*
in a sharp design –
compasses, triangle,
the open book
that might be scammed
next a steer's bum.
Each time I take a look
it reminds me of a signet ring
on a butcher's finger:
blood and coins,
the metric rod,
and a girl crying
'I don't like it now.'

Now a daylight god
has opened the sixth book
and must go down into the ground
like Achilles –
Achilles strapped in leather,
a pushy jerk
on his night journey.
I can smell his seed
and know it's wasted;
it can't belong.
While up in the world there

the roads are straight and secular,
everyone says what they mean
under the stamped sun
and the earth is bent
by blades and machines.
All I want
is to snatch a sleaked song
till a wetness slicks and grows
on your dagged black hairs
– but what nature is
and what's natural,
I can never tell just now.

The Maiden That Is Makeless

I was sitting on a wall
in Co. Clare:
dew brish on the grass
and the light knocking
each drop of it
into the coldest of lead colours –
magenta and chill purple,
quicked blues that broke
on queasy greens –
all beautiful and base
like the rings of Saturn,
or the style a platinum blonde
who'd skimmed in a jet
from Connecticut
flipped *aluminum* to me
through a hi! smile
one hour before
she took me apart
down a creashy lane.

This wet, fresh place
was all amethyst and jism,
and as I had in her hand
it melted in me
the second I slung myself
into the priest's black Morris –
what a grand day it was, sure,
and didn't that mountain
of pure, bare stone,
though it struck me then

like a pap next a missal
beyond the dark jacket,
have a special position
to his way of thinking?

The House of Jacob from
a People of Strange Language

Slips from me like a tongue
I don't want to know –
cattle-raid,
book of the tribe,
their slow sheensong
as clouds herd
through an *aisling*.

At high tide
red mullet
shoal to the creamery's
stainless downpipe.
Two men on the rocks
drop curd possets
into the warm . . .
each mumbled hook
comes dripping back.

Fivemiletown

The release of putting off
who and where we've come from,
then meeting in this room
with no clothes on –
to believe in nothing,
to be nothing.

Before you could reach out
to touch my hand
I went to the end of that first
empty motorway
in a transit van
packed with gauze sacks
of onions.
I waited in groundmist
by a hedge
that was webbed with little frost nets –
pointlessly early
and on edge,
it was like rubbing one finger
along the dulled blade
of a penknife,
then snapping it shut.
I need only go back,
though all of my life
was pitched in the risk
of seeing and touching you.

A church and a creamery,
the trope of villages
on the slow road to Enniskillen
where they made a stramash

of the Imperial Hotel
two days before
our last prime minister
was whipped to Brize Norton
at smokefall.

When I found the guest-house
opposite Byrne's Hardware
the girl, Bridie, said 'Nah,
she's not back yet –
d'you want wait on her?'
But I went off
down the main street
like the place was watching
this gaberdine stranger
who'd never seen it before.

There was a newish wood
above a small, still lough
so I climbed into its
margin of larch and chestnut,
one of those buck eejits
that feels misunderstood –
the pious, dogged friend
who's brought just comfort,
no more than that.

I smoked a cigarette
while an olive armoured car
nosed down the hill –
no more than I could, it'd never fit
the manor house's *porte cochère*
and white oriel,
for I felt dwammy sick
at the fact of meeting you again

so near and far from home
and never saying
let's run from every one of them.
There was a half-hour
when I could still
slip back to The Velma
and leave a note with her –
I called but you weren't in.
See you.

Defenester

It was silkscreen –
mid-Mahon with a tang
of Manhattan.
This ribbed worm
hung it in his bathroom
and admired
the sebumgrey frame
and the glass.
Inside was something else –
didn't exist, like the void,
though my own face
could pass
over and through it,
in love with the big bang
of Luther's Bible,
the quick smoke-trace
that was Jan Hus,
all our doctrines of horse-shit,
apples, *Schwarzerd*, remanence,
as the air whapped
like blown gas
and I cleaned my teeth
with tight white floss.

Rosetta Stone

We were real good
and got to share a desk
that smelt like the head's Bible
when I lifted up its lid
and nicked a sharp HB
from Eileen's leather pouch,
knowing that she knew
but would never tell on me.
There wasn't a single hair
between our sleeping legs
that I could ever see –
only that spiky *différance*
waiting on history.
Hers was a little plum,
mine a scaldy that could pee
yella as the tartan skirt
she slid one tiny bit
to let me touch her pumice-silk,
chalky like my glans might be.

Symbolum

after Johann Wolfgang von Goethe

The mason lives
in this or that street
and all his actions
are like yours or mine.
He makes us equal.

He sees loose clouds
like a bishop's jowls
and the furred stars
that should be even –
king superstitions.

But he'll go out
with spirit-level,
square and trowel
to plant a ladder
on this earth.

The sun shines
on his foundations –
a pentagram
cut in packed soil,
the bricks stacked ready.

Jefferson's Virginia

1   *The Give-thanks*

> No one's bid me track a cursor
> the whole winter long –
> now each dayclean a shoot flips
> like a pip of green radar
> over the Newfoundland Banks
> and for all the wet stems
> there's this wee kid who dips
> through my blossomy room –
> *sing dada, my dadar,*
> *a poppy new song.*

2   *Those Gamey Locutions*

> Why be a redneck and chew squirrel
> when you've tasted lessons
> in the prune vowel,
> the full, fake cadence?

3   *Plate Glass*

> The Swedish poet
> is reading his new work.
> It's not a problem for me –
> a team of nine men
> has glossed his typescripts
> into wried Anglish.
> Like bodyguards in cheapo suits
> they must stick around
> at this seminar on the private life.

4   *April Fool*

Aren't I the fly man
skitting over the water
like a devil's needle?
the weight of it's nothing,
and neither foxed Lord Faulkner,
Major Henry Sirr,
nor the cricket-master
in his Wicklow tent,
matter a damn this day.

Calque

I got up and went downstairs –
that was the first act
        waxy and banal
        of the day
now the entire room had this
        set smell
        cold tobacco say
except that estranged phrase
it turned me right off
like an owl had gone *cucu*
out in the cleared day
        and the light
        that light
        all cold clean buyable
        Hardware River
        wrapped in cello
        or some kinda sap
don't they all wear the same fucking clothes?
        oh my head's sore
        there's just no aura
        OK so it's repro OK
but every last bitta this is me

Were the Rosenbergs Framed
with a Pack of Jello?

I was feeling kind of feisty
that bluecold day in Taos Pueblo
when I happened on a smashed chapel
above the Indian cemetery.
Like Mr President, they sure kicked ass,
those braves, in '48,
till the US Army
started chucking shells
at the priests' stained house –
I'd say they were well rid of it.

Voronezh

(Anna Akhmatova)

You walk on permafrost
in these streets.
The town's silly and heavy
like a glass paperweight
stuck on a desk –
a wide steel one
glib as this pavement.
I trimp on ice,
the sledges skitter and slip.
Crows are crowding the poplars,
and St Peter's of Voronezh
is an acidgreen dome
fizzing in the flecked light.
The earth's stout as a bell –
it hums like that battle
on the Field of Snipes.
Lord let each poplar
take the shape of a wine-glass
and I'll make it ring
as though the priest's wed us.
But that tin lamp
on the poet's table
was watched last night –
Judas and the Word
are stalking each other
through this scroggy town
where every line has three stresses
and only the one word, *dark*.

Mythologies

I like that story with its thoughtful prisoner,
miles of salt marsh and a word like *wesh*
I could never figure –
those chalk sticks making buckled letters
              on slates the colour
              of a schoolgirl's knickers
then the sour cloth you wiped the slate with.
There was something in it, too,
              about a jack –
jack-knife, jack-towel, jack,
              words for lawyers
              perhaps
              or dead geraniums
              waiting to be topped.
I read it in my oral childhood –
              some daft ould map
              had joined the Farcet's mouth
              to the mainland
so I could cross that bridge like Satan
              and hide among
              the British people
not noticing their love of dog-smells
              fairgrounds
              pub signs
              smoked dukes
most anything at all with bottom in it.
Also the stadiums where they moan and thresh
              they moan and sigh
              like knobby forests.

For this was like an almost-love
        some love you never chose
        you wipe your nose just
        come back for more
        and print neat lies.

Where's this Big River Come From?

We were walking back along the Lagan
me and Noel Sloan,
two schoolkids wanting to be writers.
'Could you make new words up?'
he asked me, 'not puns but.'
I said that *sdark* was the only one
had ever slipped into my head.
'It's wick, though – too Nordic don't you reckon?'
I felt a bit like a bishop saying that.
Noel kept quiet, till at Queen's Bridge
he asked, 'D'you ever say *jap*?'
We could try stick it to a spat of water.

'There are many wonders on this earth'

Chorus from Antigone

There are many wonders on this earth
and man has made the most of them,
though only death has baffled him
he owns the universe, the stars,
sput satellites and great societies.

Fish pip inside his radar screens
and foals kick out of a syringe:
he bounces on the dusty moon
and chases clouds about the sky
so they can dip on sterile ground.

By pushing harder every way,
by risking everything he loves,
he makes us better, day by day:
we call this progress and it shows
we're damned near perfect!

Breez Marine

It was my birthday
in the Europort
a Polish barber
cut my hair so short
that a young squaddy
came blinking out
– chin smooth
legs unsteady –
into that glazed street
they call Coldharbour.
We waited three minutes
by the photobooth
– some early warning –
and me and her
we fought a battle
'bout my hair
and my blue passport.
She laughed at me
by that barbarous pole
so rudely forced
and when the wet prints
slid through the hole
shrieked *just as well*
we'll never marry
would y'look at those?
Each stunned eye
it shone like a dog's nose
pointing at a prison dinner.
All I could try
was turn a sly
hurt look to soften her
and that night in bed

[30]

I stuck my winedark tongue
inside her bum
her blackhaired Irish bum
repeating in my head
his father's prayer
to shite and onions.
But my summum pulchrum
said *I've had enough*
we rubbed each other up
a brave long while
that's never love.

I Am Nature

Homage to Jackson Pollock, 1912–56

I might be the real
> Leroy McCoy
> landsurveyor
> way out west
> of Gila River

you know I pushed my
> soft bap
> out her funky vulva
> her black thighs
> and my first cry
> was Scotch–Irish
> a scrake
> a scratch
> a *screighulaidh*

I passed nights
> sidewinding
> on the desert floor
> fertil arid zone
> smoke trees
> creosote bush
> ironwood
> Joshua trees

till I lit
> on dreamtime
> wrote my nose
> in sand
> the infants'
> burying-ground

I did learn for sure there
                        smoketaste
                        piñon
                        chicken flesh
                        mesquite

and turned wise
                        as sagebrush

smart as the tabs
                        on a 6-pack
                        as cat's claw
                        chickenwire
                        thorn

I flicked fast through the switches
                        licking her oils
                        blood gunge
                        paintjuice
                        gumbo
                        Stella McClure
                        off of my skin

rubbed all of them back but
                        hear me sister!
                        brother believe me!

just banging on
                        like a bee in a tin
                        like the burning bush

cracking dipping and dancing
                        like I'm the last
                        real Hurrican Higgin

[33]

critter and Cruthin
scouther and skitter
witness witness
WITNESS TREE!

11/11/84

for David Williams

'The public knows very well the distinction between wrestling and boxing; it knows that boxing is a Jansenist sport based on a demonstration of excellence.' *Roland Barthes*

They're at it again
this wick decade
the Cartesian
and his female wrestler
who's just eaten
an omelette *baveuse*
off a porcelain plate.
She looks on him
as a peeled joker
kinda tulip poplar
'at wants to poke
je sème partout
between her wet lips.
He's no limbs but
this bodiless
tight monster
you watch them flip
into a croupier's
airy feint –
M. Clemenceau
lending Woodrow Wilson
a steel cigarclipper
from the Quai d'Orsay.
Its toolsmooth light shone –
it shines still –
like the rails in the Métro.
Look they zip away

into a black hole
like a line by Mallarmé
or this cropped kid
they call him Dale
a warder's strapping
to a gurney.
Dale has nine minutes
on their deathwatch –
he shivers
delicate and brittle poor wee thing
as tinfoil.

Last Statement

(Vladimir Mayakovsky)

It's after one,
you're in the sack, I guess.
The stars are echoed
in the Volga's darkness
and I'm not fussed
or urgent anymore.
I won't be wiring you
my slogans and my kisses
in daft capitals:
we bit green chillies
and we're through.
We were like lovers
leaning from a ferry
on the White Canal –
our arguments, statistics,
our fucks and cries
notched on the calculus.
Ack, the night has jammed
each signal from the stars,
and this, this is my last
stittering, grief-splintered
call-sign to the future.
Christ, I want to wow
both history and technology . . .
I could tell it to the world right now.

Mount Stewart

I can't believe these floating letters,
not here and not now.
That some military man
should have planted his own surname
on a few sloping fields,
then had it rubbed out
by the local demotic –
it's like I touched both your breasts
that time we were lying low
in the grassy mouth of the plantation.
We'd hid from your tribe
and disappeared from ourselves
(I've heard *n'y a pas de hors-texte*
and guess Universal Man's
a simple fold in all our knowledge
comme un tout petit pli
de lin ou de toile).
But this imaginary mount
must be the Mount of Venus,
a name stuck on a Tyrone valley
that got changed to a small distance –
so it's as much my idea
as sucked sugar-cane
or falling stars and figs.
The fancy eruption
of tall finials
breaks into Elizabethan
of a whimsical
yet scholarly kind.
Scanned through the trees
that cake of yellow stone
felt more like a transmitter

than a house called Blessingbourne.
The buzz in our voices
brought blood to our cheeks –
we'd gone to ground as friends
so we touched, rolled and broke
only in speech . . .
a bit like reading
an anonymous love-letter
before it gets written.
But the town
deep in its womb of fives –
the town had no centre
so I could never figure
who'd be watching your door
on the main street.
Now, in the dream of our own plenitude,
I want to go back
and rap it as milk, jism, cinnamon,
when it might be a quick blow-job
in a 6-motel,
or a small fear just
in a small town
in Ireland or someplace.

Sure I'm a Cheat Aren't We All?

This box
Profile Ref. C.64 BRITISH EASTLIGHT Made in England
it's for real
I bought it in a stationer's on Broad Street
of course you know Broad Street
it's close to the Martyrs' Memorial
that was March 24th
1972
and I took it with me
that wide cloudless day
into the gloomy belly
of Sir Thomas Bodley

as usual there was a smell of Anglicans
and I tried ask myself why didn't I feel easy
in my own church?
but as I couldn't actually frame the question
there was no answer
so I began dropping cards into my new box
my stamped plastic box a fawn one
and it was like filling in ballot papers

Haeckel, *The Riddle of the Universe*
Die Welt als Wille und Vorstellung
Thomas Hardy at the Barber's
The Strings Are False
I filed piles of these titles
all the while hunched in a creaky wooden room
they call Duke Humphrey
a room full of real scholars
the kind that reek of cold hare and prunella

when I broke for lunch something was happening
that felt in the free crowd light and leisure
like living inside an idea a new one
for this was the day another building in another
                                        country
had its life as parliament a house of speech
suspended prorogued done away with
though I wasn't in the least happy

because you'd fallen for this young priest
he was a loiner Tim Ryan that's a lie
and driven with him July a heatwave
all through the West the East Riding
some harbour Hornsea Spurn Head it's pathetic

you were in cheesecloth he'd green shades I could
                                        scream still
the Society of Jesus White Fathers it's invisible
as that day the same day she and me
we made a heavy pretence of love
I mean we'd a drunken fuck in the afternoon
after a dockland lunch the Land of Green Ginger
its smell of sex herrings desire

and I fell asleep with the blinds drawn
waking up like a Cretan
after a dish of leveret and black olives

clammy stunned
a caked lie on my lips
and no pattern in the thing at all

or maybe only I was boxed in
maybe that sappy something we call experience

An Ulster Unionist Walks the
Streets of London

All that Friday
there was no flag –
no Union Jack,
no tricolour –
on the governor's mansion.
I waited outside the gate-lodge,
waited like a dog
in my own province
till a policeman brought me
a signed paper.
Was I meant to beg
and be grateful?
I sat on the breakfast-shuttle and I called –
I called out loud –
to the three Hebrew children
for I know at this time
there is neither prince, prophet, nor leader –
there is no power
we can call our own.
I grabbed a fast black –
ack, I caught a taxi –
to Kentish Town,
then walked the streets
like a half-foreigner
among the London Irish.
What does it feel like?
I wanted ask them –
what does it feel like
to be a child of that nation?
But I went underground
to the Strangers' House –

We vouch, they swore,
We deem, they cried,
till I said, 'Out . . .
I may go out that door
and walk the streets
searching my own people.'

From *Landsflykt*

(August Strindberg)

I heard a voice out of Europe
a southern accent
Away to hell, England,
you're so dry on the outside
dry and chalky
but your inside's like a coal barge
parked between the North Sea and the Atlantic
an island of warehouses and corner shops
– they all smell of bacon and stale bread
down with Disraeli
damn the Anglican Church
damn your pious women
who knit and make tea
damn your imperial males
all sabres and pricks
your cheapo novels your daily Godawful papers
your mission halls and Salvation Army

Then I answered out of the North
you're all beef, sin, coal, chalk
but that's no matter
don't think I'm taken in
by your lovely bottles of Pale Ale
your neat warm pubs
or your excellent razor blades
– no, I forgive you
I forgive your crimes in Africa, India, Ireland

– I'm letting you off the hook, Albion,
not for your own sake, never,
but because out of your steam presses
shot Dickens, Darwin, Spencer and Mill!

Why The Good Lord Must Persecute Me

I don't visit this noticeboard much
– the one in my study
maybe you only look at them
when you're in real need
– there's a list or a timetable
some piece of printed stuff
that orders you to do
or to be something
but I keep one picture
pinned to the black cork
– CALVIN FAREL
each theologian
is let into a wall
like a long thin clock
– fierce *féroce* feral stiff
a pair of stone pricks
or the boots I dig with
   my brain's gonging now
I've just had a liquid shite
then juice coffee a horrible suck
of black caporal
now now now I'll unfold a chair
and stare at that high terrible scooped smooth
rational wall
between my eye and the water jet
all the while I'm leafing through
The History of Received Opinions
– see this, the word *tradition*
it'll squeak if you touch it
then break up like a baked turd

into tiny wee bits
and here's a missing chapter
that tells what you can't rub out
however much you might want to

Really Naff

He'd cropped hair
and a sweater –
a tight one on bare skin.
Something too full about the face
but shy with it.
A bit like a tope –
a tope or an airplane
if you seen them from above.
There was this warning flag
at the quarry –
someone's underpants strung on a pole
by a concrete hut.
I felt the blast stub the hill
then we climbed up a track
past Lough Free they call it.
We drove home the next day.
My eyes were wide open,
I stared down –
it's the thrash of new love –
at these scribbly lines
in the Ormeau Baths.
I notched his neck with my lips.
In bed he was all thumbs –
I was jabbed like a doorbell –
until he collapsed
sticky with the promise
of making my bum.
Which he didn't.
So I call him Mr Thumb
and draw eyes on that face
with a felt tip –

flat as a pancake
or a kid's drawing.
I put in ocean, fathoms, light,
but he's as bare as need, poor guy,
or the sole of that trainer.

Are Those F-111s?

for Blake and Kathy Morrison

I crossed over Darsham Heath
– whin and warm wilderness
and found the steps to the beach
thirty-nine concrete slats
then the skreeking give of shingle
the North Sea's a flinty ochre
– wave bash bone rattle wave bash
and Sizewell's a zinc crate
between the heath and Essex
– watch me as I try lift
that heavy word *objective*
it's horned and spiny
like a mine from the last war
some rusted bolus stuck for decades
in the mouth of the River Orwell
    this morning in your vinerooted kitchen
I felt for it like a toast crumb
as some hack on the radio said George Blake
was actually a triple agent
who'd no need of a fuddled Irishman
to help him escape
– I guess before he starts breakfast
he's always to ask himself
who'll eat first, second, third?
but how the fuck could he ask
if there's no self to begin with?
it's like one of those paperbacks
we're all into trashing
– *The Integrity of the Personality*
or *How to Firm Up Your Identity*

– signposts to this terminal aporia
where I'm bluffing some grand universal
called Paul de Man or Poor Tom
and the weight of the social moment
is just breaking me up
     that rusty mine
it's purely subjective
but this heartland quops in my head
complete all of a piece
its every lane pub harbour martello
blessed by Hicks or Wallis or Anon
     now you've lent me this flintstuck
hideout and herb garden
I'll unpick the fluff from my navel
and let it drift over England

Chucking it Away

after Heine's In der Fremde

I'd a homeland at one time
– strange you weren't born there
and though the trees were few and far between
– great parks of chestnuts in Yorkshire
I fell in love with bareness wetness speech
the hazel the holm oak and the screggy hawthorn
(there was a rumour some hardriding junkers
had burnt or felled the trees to stretch their estates
and then one night I was eighteen hitching through
                                        Europe
I was taken down this autobahn into the Black Forest
the dark was packed with something I felt shit scared
something I'd no name for but it sickened me)
I was born in the Jewish quarter of a big ugly city
on the other island
and now I live just down the road from all those moors
                        and wrecked factories
– it's two nations this place you can't feel easy
though when I drive north up the A1
I find in myself a drab liking for all the poplars and diners
the windsocks and pocked hangars on the airfields
but when my kids pin a map of Ireland in their room
or sit crosslegged under a portrait of Guru Nanak
I'm twinged by different musics
– it's one thing being British
but you need a white skin to be English
then you can shout things in public places

at kids of a different complexion
and feel rooted or threatened or part of the land
while the rest of us keep our heads down feel grateful or
angry
– as to being Irish I'd like to believe
it's only the difference
between calling yourself James instead of Philip
if your name happens to be Larkin

The Defenestration of Hillsborough

Prague

Here we are on a window ledge
with the idea of race.

All our victories
were defeats really

and the tea chests in that room
aren't packed with books.

The door's locked on us
so we begin again

with cack on the sill
and *The Book of Analogies*.

It falls open at a map
of the small nations of Europe,

it has a Lutheran engraving
of Woodrow Wilson's homestead

in a cloon above Strabane,
and it tells you Tomáš Masaryk

was a locksmith's apprentice.
This means we have a choice:

either to jump or get pushed.

The Caravans on Lüneberg Heath

one of those unlucky Fridays, Simon,
    a bust-up, dirty time to be alive
writing an elegy for the pumpkin hut and *Gärtchens*
without your neat metre and full rhymes

what I have to say's dead obvious
    we've had x years of blood and shit
    and some of us have written poems
    or issued too many credos through the press

    Simplex plays the pipe indeed
    But the soldiers pay no heed.

waiting a contact watching the normals
in the quick frame of their street lives
. . . cigarette butts carriers bus passes ackhello
they lie whole weeks in attics
wire potato clamps
or kit themselves in aprons and straw hats
knowing the natural order
for the vigilant fake it is

I'm watching three young butchers
dressed up as themselves
it's a hot new lunchtime
in the town of Newry
they camp through the market look

then break triangulate gap

you'll hear the shots like instant recollection

Simplex sees the squad car stop –
Four young men have got the chop.

*

it took us a few years only to grow that house
on a bit of land the town council give us
a cultured place beside the River Pregel
where we read out poems to each other
hoping that Zion's daughter
was maybe a presence in our speech
– surely she'd help us shelter from the rain?

other people that concept we grew up with
they made us out a pack of tubes
our heads full of gourds pumpkins squashes peppers
we treated cucumbers like art objects
and loved the slippy gunge that cauls the melon seeds
every stranger was made welcome in our house
you brought a bottle or a spondee and got tight
you cast your bread upon the waters of the Pregel
and things came back to you that primal happiness
before you turned like Christ upon the mother
sangar blockhouse lookout post OP
you made a garden in its place
a cultivated man turning the earth and raking soil
till it smells like new cord and you press the seeds in

*

Simon you're the It that isn't there
you're the reader and the writer
the crowd's buzz

 a sizzly shifting block of midges

[56]

as I trailed one hand in the Pregel
or trailed it in the Pregolya
a river named during a wet lunch at Potsdam

sugar furs saltfish copper sandstone corn
so many commodities things being moved
through the Holy Roman Empire of the German Nation
hard to tell what would happen
as the Empire burst like a bag
and logs slipped downriver
to the papermills at Königsberg

how many years back were Slavata and Martinitz
pushed out of that window?
at what hour of the night was it in Ruzyn
or Hradcany Castle they hanged Slansky?
thousands of statements dropped from the presses
and the day I read Kant's starry sentence
on a bronze tablet in Kaliningrad
my protestant faith in the printed text
turned back on itself

Tilly Wallenstein the spider Spinola
Gustavus Ferdinand Charles
Colonel Horn working the Lauterbach Valley
how scrupulous the sense of landscape is
in every description of armies before a battle

the flat sandy soil scrubby woods holm oak and larch
the narrow marshy streams slick oily water
between Rocroy and Rumigny
the lagoons and salt marshes of East Prussia
Simon I sometimes believe it's us poor saps
give each of these places its strange and exact presence
as if we're part of the action though the whole bloody mess

[57]

it doesn't depend on our minds just
for the <u>chosen</u> ground is always packed
<u>with skulls in section norns some end result</u>

*

we cracked too many bottles
in our fuggy bower
we smoked and made mantalk in the small hours
we cut our girls' names on pumpkins and melons
– *Arsille Rosita Emilie*
the letters distorted as they grew
and our writing stopped being ours

cucumber leaves furred with wee spines
like glasspaper or emery skins
you could polish furniture with the dry ones
or stroke one finger over their crinkly pumice
I imagined marketing them like poems
each one the slow rub of high culture
waxing a chairback's wooden pelvis

so I dreamed and wanked in a cage of swelling vegetables
each living graffito mocking my prick's ikons
riverboats passed trailing music like vines
each name went its own way left me behind
the place is a wreck now I just hurry past it
looking for signs of age in myself the used voice
the creased pouchy face on a coathanger
understudy for that weddingcake left out in the rain

half truths cagey handshakes those lyrics written
to your own sadness and tight esteem
I cling to my friends like soft rain on bar windows
I don't believe God is much interested

in this or that country what happens or doesn't
and after twenty odd years breaking lives like firewood
is there anything can shock us now?
the Virgin of Magdeburg charred in a ditch
the sleeping girl they shot because she married out
why give a shit if what you write doesn't last?
could you feel could you really feel any joy
watching the nation states rising up like maggots?

*

the West's last thinker, part woodcutter
and part charlatan
is digging trenches on the Rhine
                    – lonely uncanny violent
                    the artist and the leader
                    without expedients
                    apolis
                    without structure and order
                    among all that is –
in the summer of '44
a memo named me the most expendable
member of my university

I was thankful digging
this will be useful to me
like an alibi
I was thinkful dagging
in the firebreak
the firebreak between armed forests
Herr Professor
must keep his head down
                    – bridge and hangar
                    stadium and factory
                    are buildings

[59]

but they're not dwellings
Bahnhof und Autobahn
Staudamn und Markethalle
sind Bauten
aber keine Wohnungen –
if I refused to drop
three Jews from the faculty
had I not praised
Totenbaum
rooftree
coffin
tree of the dead
– a farmhouse in the Black Forest
built two centuries back
by the dwelling of peasants?
as I praised the Führer
it was like all the dead feet
walked into our room
where my wife stood by the fire
cleaning my hairbrush
and I complained to her
about that thin singed aftersmell
its bony frazzle and suddenness

*

he digs deep in the earth
or stands with small tight goggles against the snowglare
a survivor like you and me
outside the ski hut at Todtnauberg
this old smooth fuck
tried stare through history
at the very worst moment

Simplex watched the committee men
Shuffle, mumble and give in.

without conscience
the day they buried Husserl's ashes
I kept to a ribbed path
and listened to the forest
its silent tidal boom
the all cave of language
and I heard him
Masaryk's teacher
as I watched the Rhine
'a wordy digger
is not the worthy digger
of his own grave
you're one of those small fry
who funked my sickroom'
days after he died
I'd written Frau Husserl
'forgive me
I should have stated
my admiration and my gratitude'
then I dropped the dedication
Sein und Zeit
was as clean as its title
a set text
the pages resinous
as pine laths
knocked into a box
and the missing name of Edmund Husserl
rosepink like a knot
or the eye of a white mouse

this red Rhine clay
lignite and gravel

Grund
I stood on the wet
ontic particles
my boots sogged
in muddy water
fires luffed
on the other bank
fires the French had lit
I bribed a guard
and hid six nights
on a mudbank in a *Totensee*
one hour before dawn
on day seven
I crossed their lines
coffee and a visa
Bolivia Paraguay anyplace
what wouldn't I have given
for just those two things?
but the lieutenant's face
was the face of a student
tensing in a seminar
der kleine Judenbube
from NYU

'Go chew acorns
Mr Heidegger
you went with the Nazis'

thrown into a place
unstable here and nowness
a forest pope who lived
on the quiet side of the stink
I answer
if others did worse
they did worse

but some felt guilt
guilt is not my subject

male corpses
floating downriver
in white winter battledress
the wide melting root
of Germany
they weren't my fault
 one hundred metres of piano wire
the July plotters
noosed in a warehouse
I might've sat in that courtroom
next Helmut Schmidt
a uniformed observer
postponing speech

I was watching the Rhine
as a sealed truck
powered by wood gas
jupped through the forest
I never saw it
nudge the gates of Flossenbürg
never watched them
take that pastor to the gallows

Bonhoeffer Bonhoeffer
is this then *meine Schulde*?

*

> *Simplex sees the final strike*
> *Devastate that evil Reich.*
> *Simplex says I'm going now*
> *You can read this anyhow.*

*

[63]

water's twisting down the hillsides in long sheets
all I can say is they fought over the same places
        Alpine passes
        Rhine crossings
        Regensburg bridgehead
        Magdeburg bridgehead
        the plains of Leipzig and Brabant
easy to say it now the war's long over
but you'll find me Simon an idea only
where five khaki caravans are parked on a heath

I'll follow in the Field Marshal's shadow
an orderly an illusion that crosses
ling tyretracks crushed grass
to feel in the left pouch of its battledress
for a pen that'll pass like a baton
from one officer to the next

we unfold ten chairs and a table
in the shabby tent by the flagpole
it's inside/outside
chill temporary
like a field latrine

he keeps their delegation waiting
then draws them up
under the Union Jack
tying back a flap
I notice three brown buds on a twig
all gummy and glycerine

von Friedeburg their naval commander
he wept during lunch I wiped glasses
and held them up to the canvas light
they signed the instrument of surrender

[64]

then lit cigarettes the way young people used to
after sex in the daytime

*

now I can get born again
as a square of tracing paper
in A B or C block

flats brickfields cindertracks
it's 9 a.m.
some Monday in February
a building by a muddy river
on a postwar island

onestorey partitioned
tacked out of hardboard
and scrap fuselage
this aluminum school
is split in four sections

lines radiate
in from each pupil
and one tight thread
links Lüneberg *Heide*
to the Clogher Valley
– provincial world history
or the seedbed of soldiers

Dill Alexander
Montgomery Alanbrooke
they're crimped on my brain tissue
like patents or postcodes
their building's the hard rectangle
that kitted me out first

[65]

as a blue British citizen

which signifies only
that this flattened trashcan
has more than enough room
for Tommy's wee collection
of aesthetic judgements
decals
further descriptions
loony tunes
or Free State referenda

so in all this melt
of incident and hot metal
there's still time to stop over
on the road to Damascus
– a light a voice patch of stamped earth
and if you ask my opinion now
I'll tell you about our musical *Kürbishütte*
then hand you a cucumber
and say it doesn't exist

Notes to poems

'Mount Stewart'

Once named Mount Stewart, Fivemiletown was founded by the Jacobean planter Sir William Stewart early in the seventeenth century. It is now so called because it is five Irish miles from the nearest villages, Clogher, Brookeborough and Tempo.

'The Caravans on Lüneberg Heath'

Simon Dach (1605–59) was professor of poetry in Königsberg and the most important figure in the Königsberg circle of poets. His poem, 'Klage über den endlichen Untergang und Ruinirung der Musicalischen Kürbs-Hütte und Gärtchens. 13. Jan. 1641', was first published in 1936. It is printed in the selection of seventeenth-century poems in Günter Grass's novella, *Das Treffen in Telgte*, which is set near the end of the Thirty Years War. 'The Caravans on Lüneberg Heath' is loosely based on Simon Dach's 'Lament over the Final Demise and Ruination of the Musical "Pumpkin Hut" and the Little Garden' and is also indebted to *The Meeting at Telgte*, Ralph Mannheim's translation of Grass's novella. Mannheim translates 'Kürbs-Hütte' as 'Cucumber Lodge/Bower' and notes the allusion to Isaiah 1:8 – 'And the daughter of Zion is left as a cottage in a vineyard, as a lodge in a garden of cucumbers, as a besieged city.' Mannheim also explains that Cucumber Lodge was an informal Königsberg literary society which used to meet in the poet Heinrich Albert's garden in a bower overgrown with cucumbers. There they would sing their own songs set to music by Albert.

I have also drawn on various essays by Martin Heidegger and on certain evasive, and probably mendacious, public statements which Heidegger issued in order to justify his conduct under the Nazi regime. I have drawn, too, on Paul Celan's poem to Heidegger, 'Todtnauberg'.